ON MY BEST DAY

Tiffany Nicole Pigée is a gifted poet and creative storyteller. Crafting ballads and symphonies with her words, she gives voice to the intimate experiences of human connection and of loss and of redemption. She focuses on creating literary landscapes to explore and confront thoughts and emotions often left unsaid.

Tiffany Nicole is the author of On My Best Day, Planet of Me Universe of Us and is currently finalizing her third poetry and prose collection for release in 2023. She lives with her husband and a growing collection of fiddle leaf figs.

ON MY BEST DAY

Poetry and Prose for the Soul

TIFFANY NICOLE PIGÉE

On My Best Day
Copyright © 2021 by Tiffany Nicole Pigée/
Maurcole Unlimited, LLC. All Rights Reserved.

Maurcole Unlimited, LLC
P.O. Box 20378
Atlanta, Georgia 30325

Maurcole Unlimited LLC fully supports copyrights. No portion of this publication may be reproduced, stored, or transmitted in any form or any means, electronically, mechanical, photocopying, digital, recording, scanning, or otherwise without the expressed written permission of the author and publisher.

Requests to the author and publisher for permission should be addressed to the following email:
inquire@sincerelytiffanynicole.com

ISBN 978-1-7375108-0-2

Printed in the United States of America

21 22 23 24 25   7 6 5 4 3 2 1

Cover Design/ Interior Design by Melvin Pigée

for my husband,

My best friend, my confidant, my partner, and my editor - there is no possibility of me being who i am without you.

for Rhina,

I imagine these pages to be everything you ever wanted to say. but ~~couldn't~~ didn't.

on my best day

yesterday. i promised myself, tomorrow
would be better. said all the right words.
gentle reminders, of what lies beneath
the layers of life i've collected. asked
the universe to deliver on its promise of
wholeness.
and happy. and love

exhausted. with this day
that never ends. running
in and out of myself. looking for me
in you. even my soul knows
it's not where it's supposed to be

today. a work in progress
still finding
still unraveling
still unfolding myself.

accepting what cannot be altered.
wreaking havoc on what remains. frantic
with excitement. at the idea of being more.
better. enough.
because,

on my best day. the one that is coming.
the one who circles in incessant orbit.
on that day,
i know.
i will discover
my most perfect love, in my own reflection.

the cyclical nature of things

sometimes the path circles back.
to the beginning. returning you
to the land of your birth. drawing you
to the one place you swore off
in your youth. cursed the dirt
entirely. and, still
the road finds clever ways
to shepherd you back
to the ground of your own inception.

but everything is different now,
and not much seems familiar.
although, nothing and everything
has changed.
because you,
are not the same

the elder women don't always teach the best life lessons

she, along with a tribe

of known and unknown women

taught you life lessons. often

of the worst kind

how to find comfort in discomfort,

to smile for attention you don't desire,

and to bury the very intuition

that would have

guided you

far, far away from here

the miscommunication of peculiar women

my mother would often say
she knew she was peculiar.
a peculiar woman
she called herself. a bold declaration.
spoken with authority, as if she was
responding to some unsaid criticism.
lingering, in the air.
a bold declaration. i accepted as fact

i am sure now, eye-to-eye we were not
on what defined her particular peculiar-ness.
believing she thought i found an oddness.
an unfitness, to her. somehow different
from what i desired. somehow peculiar,
to my expectation of her.

i wish now. that she knew
then. before her spirit escaped her body,
the preciousness of her peculiar.

this rare and uncommon thing,
to be coveted and adored,
made her the exception.
the extraordinary. woman
she was. *is.*   magic.

forever loved,
by this
peculiar woman.

the peculiar woman - *for my mother, Rhina*

i am a peculiar woman
a rare breed
manifested from magic
long steeped in majesty

when i speak
rainbows waterfall from my lips
when i walk
gold streams from the curves of my hips

i am a peculiar woman
divinely unique
fire blazes from my eyes
enchanted waters form my feet

and only the universe knows
the secrets i keep

the reason we create alter egos

i want a
spirit animal
wild and free

all the things
i'll never let myself be

there's not always enough for everyone else

why is your door always open
to those with unsavory intentions?
the ones that never come to give. or fill.
or replace.

they feast on your goodness. always
leaving with full bellies. a bounty
for their empty promises. overflowing
with stroked ego. pockets fat
with your virtue

who replenishes your well?
depleted daily. as they drink
freely. from your abundance and your famine?
and what will come of you
when all is gone. and
there is nothing left?

why it's so hard for you to get them to leave

it shouldn't be this difficult
to let someone go. not when you're ready
for something new. something different.
a fresh start. a healthy connection.

it can't possibly be this hard
on your heart. when you've finally realized
how wrong this all is.
was.
from the beginning.

and especially for the ones who never should
have made it in to begin with. the ones who
come with overwhelming baggage. wedged
into the smallest spaces, of you.

when you want them to leave
you'll be confronted. by the clutter and chaos
stored deep inside you. *the hoard.*
that now barricades them in.

left to fully comprehend

how it all got there in the first place.

because you wanted this to be quick and easy.

and painless. and really,

no one ever told you,

how it could be so painful

to let someone go

the source of self-destruction

when you're young. and now sometimes
in your middle years, especially now.
i guess

> *because age is becoming a blurred*
> *line. even if the consequences aren't*

there will be things that you'll believe
you must do. the things
you gotta get out of your system. at least,
you know, just this one time

you'll convince yourself of this, first. of course.
it's okay, because you only live once. it's only
one time. really, what harm can it do.

agonizingly misled by inner dialogue
attempting to find order
in the chaos of your thoughts.

trying to make ill-fated decisions
easier on the conscience

just remember though,
when you're doing those things. the things
you gotta get out of your system. at least,
you know, just this one time
remember, as you consume those things,
to not let them consume you too

the uselessness of regret

i reside in the grey
in the shadows
somewhere between
life and death

turned to stone
by looking back
only to realize
there was nothing left

when you finally love yourself enough to leave

the time has come
for you to leave without notice
and without notice
no packed bag or suitcase. this time

there is nothing here to take. nothing
to leave behind

you will walk. straight backed. head high.
no need for backward glances.
there are no daggers left to be thrown.
no bullets to fear. only emotional exhaustion.
invading everything.
and haunting second chances

too many crossed lines for hope to remain.
and regret escapes your heart

you will exit quietly. without argument
or demand. last words confessed long ago
there is nothing left to hear and
nothing left to say

no. the final exodus. an effortless departure
not out of spite. or because of love lost
or chances taken.
but for new love discovered

the ephemeral nature of pain

pain is not forever

though you will not remember
my words. when it comes. to you.
you will suffer
with such intensity, desperation
and longing

an emotional uprooting. it will feel like death

short-lived. a moment, soon forgotten

though you will not remember
my warning. with the universe crumbling
around you. even breath,
every inhale and every exhale, a struggle

i promise it will not last

and one day. without proclamation.
like a whisper in a passing wind,
it will disappear. like a miracle.
whisked away in secret. without notice.
and without notice.

then,
and only then
will you remember my words

what happens to the forsaken women

she bled black
from wounds left unattended
suffocating slowly
from the weight on her chest
crying tears of mold
from being overexposed
abandoned somewhere
that was not her home

in the end, you'll do just fine

it will get heavy, darling
your shoulders will grow tired
your knees will ache
and your back will fail
many times

it will get difficult, darling
your thoughts will betray you
your actions will get ahead of you
and your mind will trick you
many times

but you were made for this, darling
created entirely for this journey
not just the joy and love
and delight of life
but the harsh and the messy.
the not-so-pleasant.
that you will endure
many times

but you were made for this, darling
and in the end, after all
has been endured
you will find,
that you alone
have done just fine

**protecting your peace
comes in many forms**

protecting yourself can sometimes mean
tucking away what doesn't fit. what doesn't
feel right. what is no longer familiar.

it's giving yourself space and time
away from ill-intentions and unsolicited
opinions. and unhealthy connections.

it's the unveiling and the cutting off.

no longer waiting for permission
or approval. to create a new reality,
where you are safe
and significant.
a peaceful inspired place,
that feels like home

my best self exists in early morning

i have discovered a most special thing.
it happens, before the world
has made me undone.
as the sun ascends. and new light
provides opportunity. moments, when
i am still myself. uninhibited and confident.
simultaneously. and altogether
and i am actually *all together*.
unsoiled and unbroken, by the horrors
of the day. and my innocence
is still intact, fully. as i play
catch and release with the universe
and all its mystery. its alchemy.

complete, in my everything.
secure, in my nothingness.

the reminder you need

sometimes all you need
is a gentle reminder
that your right now
is not your forever

the subtle art of being present

it took you some time. a little too long,
i'd say. to fully understand, being present
does not equal physical presence.
that just because you are here, with me
doesn't mean that you are here. *with me.*
and when you don't allow yourself to fold
into the moment. to be immersed
and undistracted. even in the not-so-exciting
but still relevant and important times. you
missed the experience. of me. completely.
and because i was preoccupied
with the seduction of your attention. i -
too have been robbed. because,
it is because of you,
that i have missed it too

safe places can be people too

tell her. in words and actions.
it's okay to be soft and delicate
to be cared for without request.
help her wash away the world and
its accompanying expectations.

tell her in repetition.
until her heart believes it. when you say
there are no requirements
for love, here.
that she doesn't have to be
any particular thing, for anyone.
especially you

open yourself completely.
so in your transparency she can expand
into herself.
vulnerable. naked. free.
here, with you.

finding rest

in this safe space. this sanctuary

where she is loved. and protected.

because safe places

can be found in people too

love doesn't ask permission

on my worst days, i was exhausted. devoured
by regret. haunted without mercy by the men
that entombed their demons inside me.

smart women said to heal first. cleanse
your spirit. don't jump too fast into something
new. but i knew what they did not. and what
i tried not to believe. about you. i -

did everything i could to make you look away.
exposed every ugly despicable thing.
even exaggerated a little. *for effect*

still, every time you were near,
because you wouldn't stay away,
your eyes told me i was safe.
your heart became my home.
and your kiss let me know
that you would never ever leave

that funny feeling lodged in your throat is a warning

the funny. and not so funny thing
about intuition. is that it tells no lies.
it does not deceive.

only warns.
and reveals and guides and confirms,
in truth.

a constant exposition
of the revelations
that have always existed.

the ones, that have always been.
sometimes exposed,
sometimes buried.

but always there.
present,
in you

the hardest part is knowing you played a part

this time. i accept my own part
in the cutting and slicing of what once was
the whole of me. i've misplaced blame
in too many places. trying to avoid
the cruelest violation. a magnificent denial
of my own creation.

this time. i admit.
i welcomed them. the most damaged souls
allowed in, for far too long. sharp knives
and fancy plates in hand. i knew
what they came for.
the remaining pieces of me. and i felt
every bite as they feasted

this time. i confess.
my contribution, to my own undoing.
as i try to make myself whole. again

the uncomfortableness of becoming you

i don't feel like myself - she whispered

why? are you okay? - i asked

i'm not sure. these shoes are too small
all of a sudden. my skin is peeling ridiculously.
and nothing about me feels right.
- she continued

oh - i grinned

you're just becoming. shedding dead layers
of who you once were. and growing into shoes
you are meant to fill - i continued

it's uncomfortable - she moaned

it's meant to be - i replied

rushing won't get you there any faster

why are you always in a hurry?
frenzy doesn't suit you

don't you know that history
is an illusion
stories told. and retold
about souls that have departed
and can't correct
or object
and would likely
tell you to spend more time living. now
than trying to make a point
that may soon be forgotten. revised
or purposefully distorted

why so eager to get to the finish line?
what purpose will you serve when you arrive
blurred memories of a process
rushed?

how does this make sense?

wasting what can't be replaced.
the most temporary gift.
both, sacred and precious.
yet, worn thin
with mindless busyness.
that won't be remembered

did no one ever tell you
it's okay to be present. living.
breathing. evolving,
at your own pace?

maybe you weren't lost after all

there is adventure. in the midst
of the unknown
in being lost
roaming
without direction or destination
leaning into your own senses
relying solely on your intuition
forced to discover
yourself
along the way

some daughters look for their mothers in the oddest places

as long as i can remember
i longed to fill her shoes.
to be full grown. in her image. a little sway
in my hips. a slight slope in my breasts.
and of course, her perfect feet

she never wanted me to wear them. just made
me more determined. as i searched
for many things. often, nothing at all.
found her in everything.

i even discovered her essence. by chance.
in worn bras. a perfect scent. the kind
that doesn't wash away. and is hard to describe.
the kind that tells her secrets. *that she lives
in regret of mistakes long made. and hates the
things she cannot change.*

on my knees, when she is absent in mind
or person, i search. frantically.
knowing they are here. hiding.
taunting me. 5 inches and strappy
always in the back. lurking.
where she thinks i cannot reach

she is breathtaking without them. naturally
beautiful. in a way that gives everyone pause.
and because she is my mother. i often pretend
that i am too

the tip of my fingers grasp a heel.
and i feel as if i won a prize.   every time

tiny toes slip into her 8 narrows. i try to walk.
one foot forward. as i always do. but stumble.
because in her shoes, i can only be still.
at the risk of falling.
of failing.
of breaking

a mirrored glance reveals secret wishes
and subtle similarities. and i imagine
for a moment that i am her.
or at least enough of her,
that others stop asking
if i was hers and she were mine

i tuck away impossible thoughts and smile
at my reflection instead. a slight nod
to the girl looking back.
a subtle acknowledgement
of what i know i can never fully be.
her

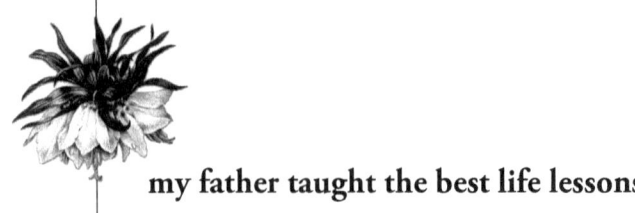

my father taught the best life lessons

actions proceed thought
and uncontrolled emotion
leads to terrible decisions
becoming ill-fated moments. and
unpleasant memories
that cannot be reconciled

a chain of chaos initiated
by mindless reaction.

no wonder my father told me
to always think.
first

**don't distort the memories -
leave them as they are**

memories are not for torment

they are gentle reminders

of what once was

only you distort them

into being

what could have been

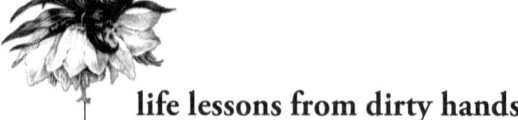

life lessons from dirty hands

there was a quaint vegetable garden, in my grandma's backyard. partially shaded, by the largest pecan tree i'd ever seen. then. or since.

the place we shared quiet moments. on early mornings. perched on our heels, knees set firm. steady.

> *i'm going to teach you something. i think you're old enough now. old enough to learn how to grow something.*

spring and most summer mornings spent in routine. preparing soil. planting seeds. watering and fertilizing the ground in seamless rotation. even when i would complain that *the dirt still just looked like dirt*. we kept working.
being patient and consistent,
until it didn't.

new buds brought other pesky things. we
pulled and plucked anything not put there by
our hands. and pruned away what didn't look
quite right or didn't grow well. and in the end,
produced a beautiful harvest

> *deny the dead and diseased the root, or lose*
> *everything. and always be sure to cut away*
> *the weak and fragile early. do this and the*
> *land will give life back to you and you will*
> *never be without or in need.*

i understand now, the seeds my grandmother
tucked away in me. on early mornings.
perched on our hells, knees set firm. steady.
how to create life and how to tend to it, so
it grows in abundance and replenishes itself.
a grandmother's wisdom

the kind of wisdom that takes root in your
soul. the kind of wisdom that, when you need
it the most, finds a way to bloom in you

when your mind's eye is wide open

the time will come. to be undone
to peel away the layers. unearthing
what has been buried. hidden.
forgotten

and you will finally
see through. to yourself

and your mind's eye will reveal
the truth. unpacking what was stored away
and your mouth
will no longer apologize
for simply being you

the beginning of me was the end of us

the truth is

the end of us. was not the end

of me.

in fact,

the end of you and i

made room for me

inside myself.

and

turns out,

endings

are not always

The End, after all.

and sometimes

finales

are beginnings too

the enemy within

of all the things my mother taught me
showed me. told me.
there were no hints. no instruction.
no life lessons. on how not to be
your own worst enemy

no warning of the damage. i'd do
to myself. the wars i'd wage
in my own mind. or the rage
that would spew from my mouth.
fiery confessions of all i wanted to change.
the things i hated. about myself

uttered words i would regret.
expressed things, better left unsaid.
better left unthought.

i hurt myself a thousand times. more
than any other.

suffered deeply, from self-inflicted
wounds. that i now know
don't always heal properly

and learning to forgive myself is a process
an entire education. a confrontation
and a reconciliation. of who i am
now. and who i've allowed
myself to be, to myself. *the enemy*

fear only has the power you give it

you alone have given up
on yourself. buried your head.
and waved a white flag long ago. surrendered
your treasure without resistance.
your soul's purpose. handed over to fear
neatly folded. and covered
in a safety blanket

balled up your power. like trash.
and scooted it across the floor.
wouldn't even shoot your shot
at the trash can in the corner.
convinced yourself you'd miss.
so you didn't even try. to stop
your mind from raging
in doubt-filled thoughts.
while your spirit died, fighting.
on fire.

a white flame. burning
in concert with the universe. in celebration

of who you were designed to be
yet here you are. *still*. a shell
of lost possibility. terrified
of your own destiny. paralyzed
by what could be. stuck.
in your mind. your own mental dam
holding everything back

sometimes the melancholy isn't so bad

something about the melancholy
draws you in. beckons to you quietly
with sad seduction and moody appeal
and who are you to deny it?

you stopped fighting it long ago.
resistance is no longer a recognizable response
and mostly, you just want to sit in it.
fuse to it. envelope yourself in it.
and release the pressure to feel. anything

and it's often subtle.
how the sorrow calls your name.
sometimes bold.
sometimes a whisper. always,
in a way,
that no one else hears.

inaudible chatter,
from the corner of the sofa
where it's soft. cozy.

a little too familiar.

and you feel hidden
and protected in this dreary cocoon.
you've discovered. free
to let go. to release.
and your tears fall
and your heart aches
and you feel at home
with the pain

let this war end

you have been damaged by a love
that didn't love you

half nursing old wounds
you won't allow to fully heal.
attempting to revive casualties
that have long expired. *relics.*
awaiting a proper burial.
the battle now lost to history.

why are you still engaging an adversary?
the one claiming this territory
as defeated. announced you as conquered
and forward marched to the next battlefield
in search of a new conquest
leaving behind victory flags.
firmly planted.
in your formerly good ground
for all to see

the thing about being suicidal

your kind words
feel more like dismissals
that echo judgement. and lack understanding

you just need a glass of wine -
a change of scenery -
a man

i beg in hushed tones
quietly explaining.
what shouldn't need words

i didn't. wouldn't. choose this feeling
of heavy and despair. this incomprehensible
weight has encompassed everything.
my whole being

these emotions strangle all desire. i suffocate
on the overwhelm. of feelings
not meant to be this abundant.
gag on infinite tears. fighting to be free

of this thing, you think
can be so easily remedied

not much is clear anymore.
thoughts murky. tainted.
and though i am most vulnerable
now. i am also most at home,
when isolated and alone.

but there is so much melancholy here.
i spend my days trying to decipher
whose thoughts are whose

and how quick you are to judge.
think i am accepting of this state of mind?
this inescapable confusion
that has invaded all of me

a war i didn't wage.
can't you see, i was ambushed
without warning. suddenly
and with force?

yet, i find myself ill-equipped and
unprepared in this battle. in this plight.
in this unrelenting mental dilemma.
in the fight for my life

we were almost diamonds

we are daughters of broken brilliance
and hidden truths. fatherless souls,
pretending to be unaffected. remnants
of our mother's transgressions.

defiled in shamed secrets.
held together by lies
we survive, only. unable to thrive
we are but a shell. empty

discarded. and ravenous. always.
and, in all ways. we crave
what we cannot obtain.
and desire what he doesn't provide

born of dysfunction.
groomed in soiled shadows.
we are coal. without pressure.
we hold no value

**the worst wounds haunt you
and never go away**

some wounds heal properly. clean
and fast. only traced by slight lines.
that make you wonder
what was once there.

others leave permanent blemishes.
the kind you can't unsee.
the ones that leave you marked
and branded. slightly damaged.
but healed, nonetheless.

and there are those that slightly scab over.
in persistent repetition. but never fully
scar. the ones that reopen
every now and then. oozing
out a surface haunting.
a seasonal reminder. the recurring trigger.
setting you on edge. then subsiding

right at your brink. tightening
into a shell of relief. a brief retreat

those are the vexing wounds.
the ones you never stop tending.
the ones you think are gone,
but always return.

the ones that live in your mind
echo in your heart
and never fully disappear

it was almost our best day

in the winter, when the air is dry
and the wind is calm. i still
think of you. and me.
ignoring the tragic parts. discarding
memories of all the harm
we did to each other

of course, it was painful.
we decimated each other, in the trying.
existing on hopeless desire.
wanting only to make it work.

star-crossed from the beginning. now,
even the good times feel tainted. by the truth
of what we weren't,
what we would never be

but it's the ache in my soul that always lures
me back in. to you.

even more. on the cold days.
just enough. to pick up the phone.
always praying for the voice
before the beep.

imagining a different ending.
knowing there is no alternate reality
to create. and that it will always be the same,
with us

self-love isn't always easy

who told you self-love would be easy?
- that the best of you
was simple. and straight. and narrow?

who said you wouldn't lose your way?
- or find yourself confused. exhausted
and disoriented. flooded with emotion
and completely undone?

the elder women know
the banshee song

hold your head back, child
way back and open wide

breathe in real deep. and release
from the pit of your soul.
the very seat of your spirit. wail,
like a banshee. announce the coming death
of what has invaded you

scream his name. full-throated
until your heart relinquishes
the poisonous seed he left behind. discarded.
purposefully abandoned

the one that seared its way
into the depths of your being
deep down. to your cursed ground.
where prayers go unanswered
and hurt and pain are watered

by tears of sorrow. fertilized
by the false truth that you are over him

you unknowingly provided
the breeding ground
and it took good root
established itself
and birthed a forest

this is a soul purge, child.
a necessary abolition

scream his name. until you taste
your own liberation. until you feel
the very essence of you, again.

scream louder, child
there's a lot of uprooting to do

a private invitation

there is heaven

in my soul

a universe of dreams

in my heart

      you should come see

this is an origin story

in my youth. i was lost in translation

everything mattered and nothing made sense.
tangled thoughts led to misguided behaviors
that escaped the grip of good manners and
proper morals

learned too early how to tip toe around
a father's rage. and how to properly
exist on a mother's essence. because although
she was present, *she had no presence*

a lifelong education in coping mechanisms
formed me into a full rebellion. a fiery riot.
disguising a hidden soul. tucked beneath
layers of us all.

entangled with spirits
that were and weren't mine.
couldn't recognize myself if i tried.
and *i did try.*

discovered in the trying, all the chaos i held.
the confusion boiling over the edge
of my insufficient pots. filled
with clouded beliefs and polluted dreams
of a life i was never meant to live

found myself pregnant with desire,
more times than i care to recall,
for an identity that failed my memories
and my imagination. even tried to give birth
to myself. again.
and once more, my spirit couldn't carry
the mayhem that warred against my truth

an exhausting journey. i relinquished all
and found my language. asked the universe
to make room for me, to embrace who i was.
to cocoon who i wasn't. and finally
to set myself free

it's okay to let go

you've been holding on for so long.
much longer than i expected.
gripping this irrational hope so tightly
that now it's choking you.

and i wonder if you understand
you are coming apart. breaking
into pieces. suffocating
slowly. under this endless pressure.

and i wonder if there's enough
of you left. in there.
to even consider
if it's really worth not just
letting go

becoming

becoming happens in the grey.
in the vast uneasiness
of not knowing what is happening.
or why. evolution takes place in the dash.
between new beginnings and final destinations.
it lives outside your comfort zone
and just beyond reach of the familiar.
the unfinished story. infinite pages
still being written.
both in and out of your control

permission

give yourself permission
to live outside the lines
to outgrow. everything
to expand
and stretch
and evolve
fully. into yourself

a constant evolution

there is always movement.
nothing ever really ceases to be.
life is an endless transition.
an unfurling mystery. energy
bursting at the seams
seeping through the cracks

even when you've convinced yourself
that nothing is happening
the universe is still expanding. around you.
through you. towards you

reach for it. grow to it. embrace it.
accept your brilliance. and come alive
in the evolution. of you

feel a little more

let your feelings rush in sometimes.
sink into them. let them overtake you
like quick sand.
all the way to the throat.
and embrace the struggle.
the sorting out.
the letting go

there is life in the feeling. in the experience
of it. let your heart fill. and empty. in rotation

it's in the ignoring and the tucking away.
and the pretending that everything is okay
that walls are erected.
and numbness devours you from within.

your inner voice, now silenced

so let your feelings rush in sometimes
let them wash over you.
like warm summer rain.

be drenched in its comfort. saturated
in love. immersed in emotion.

allow yourself to release,
to be vulnerable. open. free.
remembering only
to breathe

voluntary entrapment and other mental protections

i was trapped in my body. in my mind
to be exact. confined. willingly imprisoned.
thought it safer to be there. away
from it all. *knew that it wasn't.*

couldn't get past the doubt. but it was the fear
that held me close. captive, really.
i locked doors from the inside.
too petrified to leave.
more afraid to open up. to free myself

but the universe was calling.
kept calling. my name. specifically
and when i ignored
the knocking started. first, on one door
then, all   - again and again and again

i knew i had to answer. needed to face
what was waiting. clawing at my thoughts
from the other side of this mental prison.

knowing all along who it was.
knocking. wailing
my name. i knew
that it was me. there
now within reach. coming
to set me free

manifestation of deceit

be most careful when you're vulnerable.
lonely. open. and full of hope.
that's when they come,
with affirming words
gentle touches, and thoughtful gifts.

just as you imagined.

have you believing you manifested
exactly what you wanted

what they don't tell you about being young and free

they tell you you're young. the world is yours.
to go explore. and experience. life.
to do all the things. to feel all the feelings
with all the people. in the beautiful places.
to live without limits. *to be free*

so, you do.
and it's electric and intoxicating.
and you are easily addicted

but they don't tell you
that all of everything
is sometimes too much.
or what to do with the feelings
that come with the past,
the present, and the future loves.

the feelings that don't leave,
even when you do

or the longing. and the heartache
that comes after. for what you keep leaving
behind. for the thrill. the insatiable lust,
that you can no longer control
and is never satisfied

they don't tell you
that everything changes. but the heart
somehow stays the same. and that
in all the living you do,
you have to grieve the feelings too

a necessary slaughter

there was no different path to take.
no way to avoid the breaking.
the tearing apart.
the ruining, *of you.*

it had to be done.
a necessary slaughter.
flesh open to bone.
a clear passage to the soul.

because you needed to see.
to understand. fully.
that who you had become.
was not who you were meant to be

the hidden cost of becoming

the thing about painful experiences, *they say*,
is they teach us important lessons.
that something invaluable happens
when tribulation births wisdom.
and the worst ordeals often reveal
universal truths

but *i* say, it can't possibly be wrong.
or inconsiderate, or lacking in faith,
to wish. or to pray. or to petition.
to receive the gift of enlightenment
without the suffering. or the discomfort.
or the unbearable healing
that comes after

the shedding

you have been many. a legion.
grown in and out of the girls and women
you once were. shed skins
that no longer fit. as you parted ways
with once familiar spirits.
only to settle here.
where you find yourself
most comfortable. and free.
in love with the one. you.
you have become

the suffocating reality of memory lane

you strangle yourself daily. a soul hostage
to your own mind
and the memories that haunt it.

the things you can't alter. or undo.
regret laced recollections,
not worth the revisit

yet, you take the stroll. like clockwork
holding tight to your own neck. choking
back ghosts urgent to be free.

and your past remains your present
because your mind controls your soul.
a stronghold. refusing to release its grip

manifesting can wreak havoc on your mind

it's the routine that gets you, first.
the empty spaces of your mind you keep filling
and refilling with doubt-filled assumptions
and mindless considerations.
the most proper distractions.

as you bide the time and impatiently search
the cosmos. for a sign. something. *anything*
really, that says better days are near.
that says your petition has been answered

you wait on purpose. with intention.
burning desire and a hope filled heart.
fighting off the despair tearing at your thoughts

doing your part. with affirming words
and mantras of what could be.
and you live there.
in the wait.

because your right now, still

does not align

with what you are manifesting.

                                        but it soon will

misery loves company

they'll come see. to bear witness. when
you're the pitied thing. the tragic story.
the left behind. they'll come
with glaring eyes. that see right through.
to the vulnerability of you

they'll appear as a light. to illuminate
your path. the pied piper
of your story. luring you
with perfect melodies and empty promises.
all the while,
leading you further and further astray

pain never leaves without the last word

didn't they tell you. the women you listen to.
you can't bury the pain like you
do the memories. it will dismantle you
from the inside. each time you think
you've bottled it. it slowly seeps back
into the lump in your throat

didn't they tell you. the women you listen to.
with all their advices. you can't outrun
the discomfort. it always finds you.
a constant companion. *it won't just let you go.*

you will have to face it. open and release it.
let it speak. and it will tell you
what is required. for the process.
for the healing. for the absolution.
and when you listen. only then,
will the pain surrender
and when you listen. only then,
will it set you free

sometimes mental clarity is freedom from someone

i am finally free

no longer running

from my own thoughts

and falling into your opinions

being broken is sometimes easier

i've run in so many circles. i find myself
lost. given pieces of me to countless lovers
and it's unfortunate because i can't recall
which ones have what, anymore

and i'm too afraid to try
to remember. to gather it all
back together. to retrace my steps.
a little scared, of the reassembly. *of me.*

it's just so much easier. to live
with the fragments. and all
the broken parts. than to actually face
me in totality

love you best

on your best day,
love yourself. freely.
without audience or restriction.
be thoughtful and impressive.
take your time. find joy in exploring
your mind and body,
your interests and dreams

immerse in the loving. of you.
discover what you didn't know.
uncover what you've chosen to hide

on your best day,
love yourself. freely.
intensely, without restraint.

and come away full. whole.
complete

you have always been you

there is revelation in the process
of becoming. the learning and unlearning.
and unleashing and igniting of things.

only to reveal,
to uncover and lay bare. the truth
of what was always there

self-taught

most of life's truths, i taught myself.
like how clear thoughts and refined intuition,
void of fear and second guessing,
only exist within the absence
of other voices.

or how the alchemy of disgruntled energy
can change your home into a foreign place.
unfamiliar and ill-fitted. just walls and floors.
no longer calibrated or aligned
with your vibration.

and how the mental limitations,
the opinions and fears of others
are wildly contagious. relentless
infections. that do the most terrible damage.
of which, i've learned,

we don't always recover

**if only you knew what
i know about you**

i think. if i could. i would
wish it all away. every thing
that causes you pain.
erase the memories
that haunt your dreams at night
and the shame that keeps your eyes
low and heavy

i think. if i could. i would
make everything clear for you.
so it all makes sense.
remove the confusion
that causes you to second guess
your own thoughts and decisions

i think. if i could. i would
let you see through my eyes
how i see you.
let you feel through my soul
how i know you.
and let you experience through my heart

how i love you.

and i think then,
you would understand
your best days are near
and everything will be okay
and you, my love
will be just fine

where your spirit lives

in this temple
that holds all of you together. hold court
with the sovereign being. bow
in ~~her~~ your presence.

accept that you are divine. worthy
of worship

fall in love, once again. without reason
or hesitation. make peace
with your body. embrace this place
where your spirit lives.

inhabit all of its spaces. this is your soul's
home. this sufficient sanctuary,
a personal universe -
where only you belong

wisdom is rarely what you want and always what you need

if you find yourself with a man
that doesn't sit right with your soul, leave.
and if you have to quiet your
convictions or slow your pace for him, run.

she said it so matter-of-factly,
that i just sat there. still and silent, waiting
for more. wanting more. but that was the
sum of her wisdom on the matter. the now
blank expression painting her face, confirmed
she had said all she came to say

confused. i began to wonder if she had heard
me when i said *he was learning how to not*
hurt me. or, how *i was willing to compromise*,
for him. that i had been thinking. and,
maybe the feelings i was having, *were just me*
talking myself out of a good thing.
maybe, he *was* the one. maybe, *it was actually*
me with the problem.

maybe, she hadn't listened. fully. to me.
after all

she stood to leave, but not before taking the
last sip of blood-stained merlot, from the
gold-rimmed glass clutched tight in her right
hand. and i knew this was the last call

but, what if – i started. but didn't get to finish,
whatever it was i was about to negotiate on his
behalf. before she turned hard on her heels.
and got close. too close. her nose almost
touching my own. and hissed

*listen! those are your only choices you got, girl.
that's it! anything else and the damage is done.
hell, from the sound of it, might already be*

this time she took no chances. left no room
for my further convincing. empty wine glass
in hand, she smoothed her hair with the other,
and walked straight out the door

you are too big for the both of us

i convinced my soul that it needed less
so that i could give you more. and still,
it seems, it is not enough. because now
my thoughts hide in the shadows. always.
making room, for more of your opinions

this constant bending. subsiding. fading.
the hiding away of self. *for you*.
has left me lost. and exhausted
by the weight of your endless declaration
that you are right. and i –
am tired. and i relinquish all. *of me*

wave a white flag. high.
as i back into a corner.

shrinking. to give you space
to be bigger. more important.
all spread out, *inside me*. abundant

here, in my temple
where my spirit resides

i imagine, you will take up the room soon.
hell, the whole damn house.
until, there is little left
of me. and there is only you

**sometimes a broken heart
isn't really broken**

i thought there was a void

when you left

but discovered it was just the hole

an empty space

you burned through my heart

right down to my soul

a simple truth

i loved myself, *more*
before, i knew you

fixer upper

i was tiny shards of glass
scattered. burnt ash and sand
swept away by wind

i was everywhere
i was nowhere
shattered and destroyed
couldn't put myself back together

thought i was irrevocably broken

until you came
you saw what i was meant to be

and you walked to the ends of the earth
to find every remnant
that was rightfully mine

and glass became windows
and ash became wood
and sand became beaches

and...

there i stood

the best days save all the others

some days, it all comes together.
i know exactly who i am. and what i'm doing.
i even think i know why i'm here.

convince myself of my own importance

other days, i'm mentally and emotionally
assaulted with what i cannot control. and
the things i didn't plan for

most days, i linger. somewhere
in the middle. accepting
that everything is temporary.
that good will collide with bad.
and sometimes i won't handle
any of it right. but,

on my best days, i give myself permission
to just be. to embrace
that i am not always
the problem or the solution.

remembering that peace
can emerge from stillness. and
on these days. my very best days,
i know,
i'll be just fine.

thank you

You are here. You've completed this poetic journey with me and I am so very grateful to have shared this collection with you.

If you've enjoyed this book, please leave a 5-star review on the site where your purchased your copy or on sincerelytiffanynicole.com. I read every review and repost every photo submitted. But even more importantly, each review helps new readers discover my books.

Let's continue the journey. Don't miss reader exclusives, sneak peaks, special announcements, or book updates. Sign up to keep in touch at:
sincerelytiffanynicole.com

Follow me: Instagram: @sincerelytiffanynicole

www.ingramcontent.com/pod-product-compliance
Lightning Source LLC
Chambersburg PA
CBHW070925080526
44589CB00013B/1433